Mind Your Spelling

2

by Sue Palmer and Peter Brinton

LONGMAN

Contents

Introductory Unit

If you have used *Mind Your Spelling 1* you will know that spelling and handwriting go hand in hand.
It helps you to learn the spelling of words if you practise them in joined up writing. So this book teaches you spelling and handwriting at the same time.

In each unit we introduce you to a spelling rule.

Sometimes it's a letter string.

edge

Sometimes it's a silent letter.

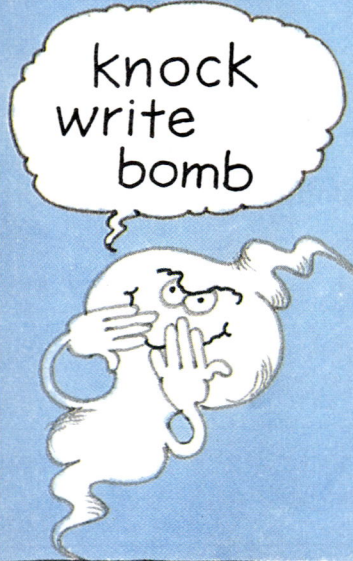

knock
write
bomb

Sometimes it's a rule about how words can be changed.

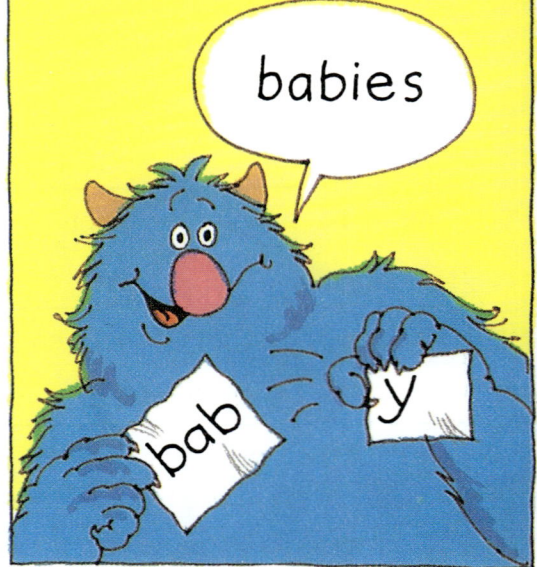

babies

bab y

Often it's something to do with the *vowels*.

Hello, we're the vowels.

a e i o u

These five letters are the vowels, and they are the most important letters in the alphabet. You will find at least one vowel in every word you write. The other letters are called consonants.

Hey, what about me? I'm special. I'm a part-time vowel.

bcdfghjklmnpqrstvwxyz

aeiou y

The letter **Y** is a part time-vowel. Sometimes **Y** stands in for a vowel in a word.

There are eighteen units in this book. Each unit will teach you one or two spelling rules.

First, make sure you understand each rule so you know what to remember in your spelling.

We'll give you lots of help.

Then try our handwriting exercises to practise the words in your best joined-up handwriting.

Don't just copy the handwriting. <u>Look</u> at each word or sentence and <u>say</u> it clearly to yourself. Then <u>cover</u> it up and write it without looking back. Then you can <u>check</u> to see if you've spelled it correctly.

LOOK   SAY   COVER   WRITE   CHECK

GOOD LUCK   **GOOD WRITING**   **GOOD SPELLING**

5

1 The oi and oy Letter Strings

Here are two vowels getting together to attract attention!

OI! OI!

We like to use our **voi**ces!

IA   oi

1 oil oil oil soil soil soil
2 boil boil boil spoil spoil
3 voice voice voice voice
4 choice choice choice choice
5 You can have a choice of
   oil paints or powder paints.
6 Don't spoil your voice by
   shouting.

Some more **oi** words for you.

And more chances for us to be n**oi**sy!

IB   oi

1 join join join coin coin coin
2 joint joint point point point
3 noise noise noise noise noise
4 noisy noisy noisy noisy noisy
5 What's the point of being
   noisy?
6 Join in the noise and find out!

We make the same sound as **oi**.

1C   oy
1. boy boy boy toy toy toy
2. joy joy joy enjoy enjoy
3. destroy destroy destroy
4. employ employ annoy annoy
5. The boy enjoyed his new toy.
6. I would not employ anyone who annoyed me.

But usually at the ends of words.
OY! OY!

Watch out for **oi** and **oy** words in your writing!

Do you remember these tricky spellings from Book One?

1D   Do you remember?
1. friend friend friend friend
2. again again again again
3. many many any any any
4. use use use used used used
5. I'll see my friend again on Friday.
6. It used to be noisy here but there isn't any noise now
7. Too many cooks spoil the broth.

Look at the Spelling

Do this work in your spelling pages.

1. Draw four columns and label them:

oil	oin	oice	ois

   Write at least two words from Unit 1 into each column.

2. The word **choice** has **ice** in it.

   a) what other word from the unit has **ice** in it?
   b) which two words from the unit have **is** in them?
   c) which four words have **oil** in them?

3. Copy these sentences, and choose the best words from 1C to fill the spaces:

   a) The _ _ _   bought a Transformer at the _ _ _ shop.
   b) I _ _ _ _ _ _ watching T.V.
   c) Please don't _ _ _ _ _ _ _ my sandcastle!
   d) When you _ _ _ _ _ _ _ someone, you get them to work for you.

4. Here is part of a letter with four spelling mistakes in it. Find the spelling mistakes and write out the correct versions.

   I made a new freind on holiday and I hope to see him agian next year. We made a castle on the beach and we yoused shells to decorate it – there were meny sorts of shells there.

5. Make up sentences of your own to include these words.
   friend   again   many   used

2 The aw and au Letter Strings

Here are two more letters that are often seen together.

I like holding your p**aw**!

Aw! Don't embarrass me!

2A   aw

1 saw saw saw straw straw
2 paw paw paw claw claw
3 law law law lawn lawn
4 yawn yawn dawn dawn
5 Cats have claws on their paws.
6 When you cut the lawn the grass dries into straw.
7 At dawn I wake up with a yawn.

You are **awful.**

2B   aw

1 awful awful awful awful
2 awkward awkward awkward
3 draw draw drawing drawing
4 drawer drawer drawer drawer
5 The drawer was stuck at an awkward angle.
6 I enjoy drawing but my pictures are awful.

Sometimes A and U make the same sound as **aw.**

But we're not often found at the ends of words.

2C au

1 cause cause cause cause
2 because because because
3 pause pause pause pause
4 sausage sausage sausage
5 Hurry up because there
   are sausages for dinner.
6 There was a pause because
   I had forgotten what to say.

au

2D au

1 autumn autumn autumn
2 August August August
3 sauce sauce saucer saucer
4 haunt haunt haunted haunted
5 In autumn the ghost came
   to the haunted house.
6 Don't put tomato sauce in
   your saucer (except in August).

Watch out for **aw** and **au** words in your writing.

Look at the spelling

Do this work in your spelling pages.

Write the heading: **aw** and **au**

1. Draw two columns and label them.

aw	awn

   Write at least three words in each column.

2. Write out these meanings, then write the best word from 2B beside each one.

   a) a picture
   b) terrible
   c) something you do with pencil or crayons
   d) used to keep things in
   e) not graceful

3. The word *awkward* is an awkward word to write. Write it neatly, then go over the **w**'s in a bright colour.

   awkward

4. Three of the words in 2C have the word *use* at the end. Find them and write them out. Go over the *use* in a bright colour.

5. Draw a picture of a *sausage* on a *saucer* with a blob of tomato *sauce* beside it. Draw arrows to the things underlined in this description, and label them on your drawing.

6. Choose the best words from 2C and 2D to fill the gaps in these sentences:

   1) July is the month before _ _ _ _ _ _.
   2) When you are writing you can use a comma to show a _ _ _ _ _.
   3) The seasons are: spring, summer, _ _ _ _ _ _, winter.
   4) A flying _ _ _ _ _ _ is known as a UFO.
   5) I love my teacher _ _ _ _ _ _ _ he/she is kind and good.

11

3 The ough Letter String

The **ough** letter string is one of the most common.

It can make lots of different sounds.

ough

3A   sounds like "uff"
1 rough rough rough rough
2 tough tough tough tough
3 enough enough enough
4 The sea was rough.
5 The steak was tough.
6 The boy wasn't rough and tough enough to join the gang.

Here's **ough** again.

ough

Making another sound!

3B   sounds like "oh"
1 dough dough dough dough
2 though though though though
3 although although although
4 We made dough to make bread.
5 I watched the programme, though I should have been in bed.
6 He enjoyed the book although it was very long.

And another sound!

3C   with a "t" on the end
1 ought ought bought bought
2 brought brought fought fought
3 thought thought thought thought
4 The boys fought because they thought it was brave.
5 They ought to have talked it over instead.
6 Have you brought the sweets we bought at the shop?

And three more sounds!

ough

3D   "off", "ow" and "oo"
1 cough cough trough trough
2 You can buy cough sweets to help make your cough go away.
3 Pigs eat from a trough.
4 bough bough plough plough
5 The kite stuck on the bough of a tree.
6 Farmers plough fields.
7 through through through through
8 The train went through a tunnel.

Look at the Spelling

Do this work in your spelling pages.

Write the heading: The **ough** letter string

1. Copy this chart and fill the **ough** words from Unit 3 into the correct places.

    Words that have the sound –

uff	oh	aw	off	ow	oo
3 words	3 words	5 words	1 word	2 words	1 word

2. Copy these sentences, filling the best **ough** words into each of the spaces.

    a) The knights _ _ _ _ _ _ a duel.

    b) The boy had a bad _ _ _ _ _ so he had to suck throat sweets.

    c) Before you can cook the bread, you have to wait for the _ _ _ _ _ to rise.

    d) I wanted to buy a bike but I didn't have _ _ _ _ _ _ money.

    e) The farmer put the animals' food in the _ _ _ _ _ _ _.

3. There are five **ought** words. Make up a little poem which uses some of them as its rhyming words.

4. The first **ough** word in the unit is *rough.*

    a) Use the word *rough* in a sentence.

    b) Look through all the other words in the unit and find one which has got rough in it. Write it down.

    c) Use the word you just wrote down in a sentence.

5. Work with a partner. Close all your books so that you can't see any of the words we have been practising.
Make a list of as many **ough** words as you can remember between you. (There are 16 given in the unit.)

4 The tch and ie Letter Strings

The **tch** letter string appears in lots of common words.

Wa**tch** out for it!

4A   tch
1 catch catch catch match match
2 snatch snatch patch patch
3 latch latch hatch hatch hatch
4 watch watch watch watch
5 He took a very good catch in the cricket match.
6 I checked my watch because I like to watch T.V. at five o'clock.

4B   tch
1 fetch fetch fetch sketch sketch
2 hutch hutch hutch crutch crutch
3 pitch pitch pitch witch witch
4 itch itch itch kitchen kitchen
5 The witch had an awful itch.
6 I made a sketch of the kitchen.
7 Fetch the rabbit from his hutch.

But watch out for four words that don't have a **t** – much, such, rich, which!

The letter string **ie** also crops up in a lot of common words.

4C   **ie**

1 field field field field field
2 shield shield shield shield
3 chief chief chief chief chief
4 thief thief thief thief thief
5 The thief stole a shield.
6 The chief of police found the
   shield in a field.

The **ie** often makes an **ee** sound.

4D   **ie**

1 piece piece piece piece piece
2 niece niece niece niece niece
3 believe believe believe believe
4 friend friend friend friend
5 I gave my friend a piece
   of pie.
6 He would not believe that
   the girl was my niece.

Look at the Spelling

Do this work in you spelling pages.

Write the heading: The **tch** letter string

1. Draw five columns and label them with the five vowels.

a	e	i	o	u
			notch	

Write as many **tch** words in each column as you can find.

2. Choose the best **tch** words from 4A and 4B to fill the gaps in these sentences.

   a) He struck the _ _ _ _ _ to set light to the bonfire.
   b) The _ _ _ _ _ cast a terrible spell.
   c) Please _ _ _ _ _ _ the kettle from the _ _ _ _ _ _ _ _.
   d) I _ _ _ _ _ _ T.V. most evenings.

How do you make a witch itch?

Take away the w.

Write the heading: The **ie** letter string

3. Draw three columns and label them like this:

ield	ief	iece

Write two words from 4C and 4D in each column.

4. Make up a short story (as silly as you like) using these five words.

   chief   thief   field   shield   niece

   Underline the **ie** in each of the words.

5. a) Never bel<u>ie</u>ve a l<u>ie</u>.
      Copy out this sentence. Use a red pencil to go over the letters we have underlined.

   b) I see my fr<u>ie</u>nd on Fr<u>i</u>day.
      Copy out this sentence. Use a red pencil to go over the letters we have underlined.

17

VOWELS – short and long

Vowels are the most important letters in the alphabet. Every word in the English language contains at least one vowel (or the letter **y,** which is a part-time vowel).

Every vowel can make lots of different sorts of sounds, by joining up with other letters.

But the most common sounds the vowels make are known as *short vowel sounds.*

These are the *short vowel sounds.*

ă as in bat
ĕ as in bed
ĭ as in chip
ŏ as in cot
ŭ as in sum

We can show that a vowel has a *short vowel sound* by putting a ˘ mark over it.

Try putting each of the five short vowel sounds between these letters to make five different words: **b_g**

Think of some other words with short vowel sounds in them.

Another common sound the vowels can make is the *long vowel sound.* The *long vowel sound* is the same as the alphabet name of the vowel.

ā as in gate
ē as in me
ī as in time
ō as in go
ū as in tube

We can show that a vowel has a long sound by putting a ˉ mark over it.

All the words in these boxes have vowels in the middle.
Which vowels are short and which are long?

hat	hate
man	mane
back	bake

bit	bite
pin	pine
lick	like

cut	cute
tub	tube
duck	duke

pet	Pete
peck	Peke

not	note
cod	code
block	bloke

Work with a partner to make charts like the ones below and
write the words from the boxes in the correct places.

a	
short	long

e	
short	long

i	
short	long

o	
short	long

u	
short	long

With your partner, find more words to fit in each column of
your chart.

5 Silent e

A silent **e** on the end of a word can change a short vowel sound into a long vowel sound. Look at these words.

Shhh. I keep quiet but I'm very important to the spelling.

5A   a-e words

1 măt → māte   2 tăp → tāpe
  fat → fate   cap → cape
  hat → hate   scrap → scrape
3 măn → māne   4 măd → māde
  pan → pane   fad → fade
  can → cane
5 Don't scrape that pane of glass.
6 Superman wears a cape.
7 A lion has a mane.

Here's silent **e** again, changing short vowel sounds to long vowel sounds.

5B   i-e words

1 pĭp → pīpe   2 pĭn → pīne
  rip → ripe   fin → fine
  trip → tripe   win → wine
                    spin → spine
3 bĭt → bīte   4 rĭd → rīde
  spit → spite   slid → slide
  quit → quite
5 You can spin and slide on a fairground ride.

In these words short vowels need a **ck** letter string.

But long vowels need **k** and a silent **e.**

5C   ck – ke

1 băck – bāke   2 lĭck – līke
  sack – sake   trick – trike
  snack – snake   pick – pike
  shack – shake   Mick – Mike

3 Old Mick kept a snake in his shack by the lake.
4 He went fishing for pike.
5 Little Mike got a trike for his birthday and he liked it very much.

Lots of longer words end in silent **e.**

5D   More "silent e" words

1 escape escape awake awake
2 polite polite invite invite
3 decide decide decide decide
4 surprise surprise surprise
5 He decided to escape.
6 I was surprised to be invited to the party.

Look out for words ending in silent e.

21

Look at the Spelling.

Do this work in your spelling pages.

Write the heading: Silent **e**

1. Copy this chart and fill in the missing words:

ă	ā	ĭ	ī
mat		pip	
hat			ripe
	fate	trip	
tap		pin	
	cape		fine
scrap		win	
	mane	spin	
pan			bite
can		spit	
	made	quit	
fad			ride
		slid	

2. These pairs of words fit into the sentences beside them. Copy the sentences and fit the best word into each space.

   a) hat, hate.　　　　I _____ wearing my ___.
   b) win, wine.　　　　Dad was trying to ___ a bottle of _____.
   c) quit, quite.　　　You should not _____ until you are _____ tired.
   d) scrap, scrape　　We tried to _____ the dirt off the piece of _____ metal.

3. Copy these sentences, putting the best words from 5C in the spaces.

   a) I _ _ _ _ _ Saturdays.
   b) You _ _ _ _ ice lollies.
   c) The boy played a _ _ _ _ _ on his friend.
   d) A _ _ _ _ _ _ has three wheels.
   e) A _ _ _ _ _ _ is a little hut.

4. Use each of the six words from 5C in a sentence of your own. You may use them in any order.

6 Silent e again

Here's silent **e** up to his tricks again.

Sitting on the end of a word making a short vowel sound into a long vowel sound.

6A   o - e words

1 cŏd → cōde   2 hŏp → hōpe
  rod → rode   pop → pope
  not → note   rŏb → robe
3 smock → smoke
  block → bloke
4 The Pope wears long robes.
5 I hope that bloke does not smoke.
6 A message in code was carved
  on the stone block.

Don't forget the **ck** letter string!

6B   u - e words

1 cub → cube   2 cut → cute
  tub → tube   hug → huge
  plum → plume
3 luck → Luke
4 The old wolf was huge but
  her cub was little and cute.
5 The lucky dice were cube-shaped.
6 Luke wore a plume in his hat.

More silent **e** words.

Can you hear how it changes the **u** sound?

long sound

Notice how silent **e** affects these words.

6C   clothes and use
1 clŏth → clōthe   cloth → clothe
2 People clothe themselves in
   cloth.
3 clothes clothes clothes clothes
4 Clothes are made of cloth.
5 us → use   us → use   us → use
6 People use cloth to make clothes.

Here are some more common words where silent **e** gives a long vowel sound at the end.

6D   More "silent e" words
1 broke broke spoke spoke
2 suppose suppose suppose
3 refuse refuse refuse refuse
4 include include include
5 I spoke to him but he was
   rude and refused to answer.
6 I suppose he's cross because
   he broke his bike.
7 The cost of the meal includes
   a cup of tea.

Look at the Spelling

Do this work in your spelling pages.

Write the heading: More silent **e** words

1. Copy these charts and fill in the missing words.

ŏ	ō	ŭ	ū
cod	code	cub	
	rode		tube
not			cute
pop		plum	
	robe	hug	
smock			Luke
	bloke		

2. Fit each pair of words into the correct spaces in the sentences.

   not   note   He could _ _ _ sing a _ _ _ _ _.

   hop   hope   I _ _ _ _ _ you can play _ _ _ _-scotch.

   tub   tube   We bought a _ _ _ of yoghurt and a _ _ _ _ of toothpaste.

   smock   smoke   A lady in a _ _ _ _ _ _ asked a man not to _ _ _ _ _ _.

   hug   huge   Gran made us a _ _ _ _ _ cake so we thanked her with a _ _ _.

3. Use these pairs of words in sentences of your own.

   cloths   clothes

   us   use

4. Here is part of a letter with *six* spelling mistakes in it. Find the spelling mistakes and write out the correct versions.

   I spent all my money so I'm brock now, and I supose Mum will refuss to give me any more. But I spock to my gran on the phone last night and she says she'll inclood a fiver in her next letter. So maybe I'll be able to get those new cloths after all.

7 Soft c

Here's silent **e** again, but this time he's up to another trick, softening **c**'s!

I can make **c** into a soft sound, like **s**.

7A ce at the end
1 race race place place place
2 face face palace palace
3 ice ice nice nice rice rice
4 police police notice notice
5 The palace is a nice place.
6 The police put up a notice about the danger of ice.

Here's soft **c** in a letter string.

nce

7B nce at the end
1 fence fence sentence sentence
2 dance dance instance instance
3 since since since prince prince
4 once once once entrance entrance
5 Once upon a time there was a prince. Ever since he was a baby he had loved to dance in strange places. For instance he used to dance on the fence.

Guess who's doing the softening!

And **e** can soften **c** at the beginning of a word too, or in the middle.

7C ce
1. cent cent century century
2. December December December
3. certain certain certain
4. except except except except
5. There are a hundred cents in a dollar and a hundred years in a century.
6. Are you certain it is December?
7. I like T.V. except for the news.

And **i** and **y** can soften a **c** as well!

7D ci and cy
1. decide decide decide decide
2. city city city pencil pencil
3. circus circus circle circle
4. cycle cycle bicycle bicycle
5. I like to cycle on my bicycle.
6. The circus ring is a circle.
7. Have you decided which pencil to use?

Watch out for soft **c** words. How many can you find?

Look at the Spelling

Do this work in your spelling pages.

Write the heading: Soft **c**

1. a) Four of the words in 7A have *ace* in them.
   Find them and write them out.
   b) Five of the words from 7A have *ice* in them.
   Find them and write them out.

2. Copy this chart and fill the words from 7B into the correct spaces.

ance	ence	ince	once

3. Copy this chart and fill the words from 7C and 7D into the correct spaces.

ce	ci	cy

4. Write out these meanings, then write the correct word from 7C beside each one.

   a) a hundred years
   b) the last month of the year
   c) absolutely sure
   d) not including
   e) a hundredth of a dollar

5. Use a pencil to draw two circles, and add a saddle and handlebars to make it a drawing of a bicycle.
   Underneath it list the three words from 7D which are included in these instructions.

6. de<u>ci</u>de
   Copy out this word, using a coloured pencil to write the letters we have underlined.
   Then use the word in a sentence.

7. Copy and complete.
   The letter **c** can have a soft sound (like **s**) if it is followed by the letter _, _ or _.

8 Soft g

Silent **e** can make a **g** soft too.

I can make **g** sound like **j**.

8A   ge

1 gentle gentle gentleman
2 German German Germany
3 huge huge large large
4 charge charge charge
5 The gentleman was a German from Germany.
6 He was in charge of a large dog with huge feet.

A common letter string is **age**.

8B   age at the end

1 age cage page rage stage
2 manage manage manage
3 damage damage garage garage
4 village village bandage bandage
5 He wore a bandage round his damaged arm.
6 Can you manage to grow a cabbage in a garage?

With my soft **g**.

And **ange** is another letter string.

8C   ange
1 angel angel change change
2 strange strange stranger stranger
3 danger danger danger danger
4 ranger ranger exchange exchange
5 There can be danger in strange places.
6 I exchanged a five pound note for change.

We sometimes make a **g** soft too!

8D   gi and gy
1 ginger ginger magic magic
2 engine engine engine engine
3 giant giant giant giant
4 Egypt Egypt gypsy gypsy
5 The railway engine was magic, and it took us to Egypt.
6 We saw giant pyramids and drank ginger beer.

GINGER BEER

GINGER BEER

Look out for words with soft **g** in them. How many can you find?

Look at the Spelling

Do this work in your spelling pages.

Write the heading: Soft **g**

1. Copy these sentences, filling the best word from 8A into each of the spaces.

   a) How much do they _ _ _ _ _ _ for an hour in the swimming pool?
   b) Be _ _ _ _ _ _ with that little kitten.
   c) A lady and a _ _ _ _ _ _ _ _ _ were standing at the door.
   d) Berlin is a city in _ _ _ _ _ _ _.
   e) The mountain was _ _ _ _.
   f) We bought a _ _ _ _ _ carton of milk.

2. Word sums with the **age** letter string.

   c + **age** = **cage**
   man + **age** = **manage**

   Write the other words from 8B in the same way.

3. Make up a little story using all of these words.

   cabbage   bandage   garage   manage

4. Copy and complete these poems, using words from 8C.

   Remember all the warnings
   Of where there might be _ _ _ _ _ _:
   Look carefully when crossing roads,
   And *don't* go with a _ _ _ _ _ _ _ _.

   When mum went out to buy our lunch
   She thought we'd like a _ _ _ _ _ _;
   She bought us sunflower seeds to munch,
   I think our mum is _ _ _ _ _ _ _!

5. Copy and complete this chart with words from Unit 8.

starts with **gi**	ends with **ger**	**gy** somewhere	**gi** in the middle
2 words	3 words	2 words	2 words

31

short AND long vowels again

a e o i u

ă as in bat	ā as in gate
ĕ as in bed	ē as in me
ĭ as in chip	ī as in time
ŏ as in cot	ō as in go
ŭ as in sun	ū as in tube

a e i o u

The words in these boxes all **begin** with vowels. Which vowels are short and which are long?

apple	age
at	ace
ale	angry
apron	and

egg	even
evil	extra
end	eat
emu	elf

ice	ink
is	I
igloo	ivy
island	in

odd	old
open	otter
ostrich	over
ocean	on

up	use
under	uniform
ugly	usual
universe	umbrella

Work with a partner to make charts like the ones below and write the words from the boxes in the correct places.

a	
short	long

e	
short	long

i	
short	long

o	
short	long

u	
short	long

With your partner, find more words to fit in each column of your chart.

Look at the words underlined in these two sentences.

    a) I <u>hoped</u> it would soon be Christmas.

    b) The robin <u>hopped</u> from branch to branch.

Which of the underlined words has a short vowel and which has a long vowel?

What about these?

    a) We are <u>hoping</u> for a white Christmas.

    b) The robin is <u>hopping</u> about.

A *double consonant* after a vowel keeps the vowel short.

ă	
fatter	patting
apple	scrapped

ĕ	
better	letting
pepper	stepping

ĭ	
bitter	sitting
ripple	sipping

ŏ	
bottle	rotten
hopping	shopping

ŭ	
butter	shutter
supper	rudder

A vowel followed by a *single consonant* and then *another vowel* is usually long.

ā	
fate	hating
blaming	scraped

ē	
emu	even
these	Peter

ī	
biting	writing
ripest	piper

ō	
coded	coped
hoping	sloping

ū	
tubing	cuter
super	ruder

With your partner, put all the words from the ten boxes above into the correct places in your chart.

9 The Short Vowel Sound and Double Letters

Remember that a double consonant will keep the vowel short.

9A double letters

1 fat fatter
  fit fitter
  let letter
  bet better

2 run runner
  win winner
  man manner
  din dinner

3 big bigger
  dig digger
  swim swimmer
  dim dimmer

4 hot hotter
  pot potter
  pat patter
  mat matter

5 The fitter runner will be the winner.

6 Please show better manners when eating your dinner.

9B double letters

1 sun sunny
  fun funny
  bun bunny

2 hot hottest
  fat fattest
  wet wettest

3 sad saddle
  pad paddle
  cat cattle
  lit little

4 dad daddy
  mum mummy
  gran granny

5 We went for a little paddle on the hottest day of summer.

6 The funny little bunny had lost his daddy and his mummy!

Here are more examples of double consonants.

If you want to keep a vowel short when adding **ing** remember to double.

9C double letters

1. knit knitting
   sit sitting
   spit spitting
   fit fitting

2. shop shopping
   hop hopping
   stop stopping
   pop popping

3. run running
   plan planning
   fan fanning
   pin pinning

4. tug tugging
   shrug shrugging
   dig digging
   beg begging

5. The man was sitting knitting and his wife was planning the shopping.

6. Try hopping without stopping running.

And if you want to keep a vowel short when adding **ed** remember to double again.

9D double letters

1. clap clapped
   flap flapped
   wrap wrapped

2. spot spotted
   knot knotted
   rot rotted

3. dab dabbed
   stab stabbed
   grab grabbed

4. skip skipped
   rip ripped
   drip dripped

5. He wrapped his things in a spotted handkerchief and knotted it to a stick.

Look at the Spelling

Do this work in your spelling pages.

Write the heading: Doubling for short vowels

1. Copy and complete this chart, *doubling letters* where you need to do so.

	add **ing**	add **er**	add **ed**	add **est**	add **y**
bat				—	
hit			—	—	—
swim			—	—	—
fit					—
sun		—		—	
pot				—	
wet					—

2. Write out these sentences, making all the words in brackets (verbs) end in **ing**.

   a) He was (sit) (chat) to his friend.
   b) I like (swim) and (run).
   c) He was (sob) and (rub) his eyes.
   d) She is (wrap) the presents and (knot) the string.

Don't forget to take the **e** off!

3. Copy and complete these charts, doubling letters where you need to do so.

	1. add **ing**
hop	
cop	
scrap	
pin	
bid	
tap	

	2. add **ing**
hope	
cope	
scrape	
pine	
bite	
tape	

Can you tell the difference between the **ing** words in column 1 and the **ing** words in column 2? If not, look back to page 32, (Short and Long Vowels Again) and work out where you've gone wrong.

10 The dge and ex Letter String

Watch out for the **dge** letter string.

dge

10A   dge

1 bridge bridge bridge bridge
2 edge edge edge ledge ledge
3 wedge wedge hedge hedge
4 hedgehog hedgehog hedgehog
5 The hedgehog stood on the bridge.
6 Don't go too near the edge of the ledge or you'll fall off.

10B   dge

1 badge badge badger badger
2 dodge dodge lodger lodger
3 judge judge nudge nudge
4 budge budge fudge fudge
5 A lodger stays in somebody's house.
6 The judge is very keen on fudge.
7 The badger wouldn't budge.

The letter string **ex** is often found at the beginnings of words.

10C ex

1 explore explore explore
2 exam exam exam exam
3 example example example
4 next next next next next
5 In the exam we had to give an example of our writing.
6 I've explored the North Pole. Where shall I go next?

10D ex

1 excite excite excitement
2 exciting exciting exciting
3 except except except except
4 expect expect expect expect
5 The film was very exciting — plenty of excitement.
6 I expect you like sweets?
7 All except fudge.

Look at the spelling

Do this work in your spelling pages.

Write the heading: **dge**

1. Draw five columns, and label them with the five short vowels:

a	e	i	o	u

Write as many **dge** words in each column as you can find (e.g. bridge would go in the **i** column because it is an **idge** word).

2. cadge   cage

   One of these words has a *short* vowel **a** and the other has a *long* vowel **a**. Work out which is which and then copy and complete this sentence.

   Cadge has a _____ vowel **a** and cage has a _____ vowel **a**.

   Can you work out why this is?

Write the heading: **ex**

3. We use the letter X to mean *kisses* at the end of a letter. If you try saying the word *kiss* without the **i** sound you will find out why.
   Write these three **ex** words and go over the x in a bright colour each time to make it stand out.

   exam   exit   next

4. Choose the best **ex** words from 10 C and 10D to fill the gaps in these sentences.

   a) I like to _ _ _ _ _ _ _ new places.
   b) Christmas is an _ _ _ _ _ _ _ _ _ time.
   c) Teachers sometimes give you an _ _ _ _ to check your work.
   d) A buttercup is an _ _ _ _ _ _ _ _ of a wild flower.
   e) Everybody _ _ _ _ _ _ _ Jamie came to my party.

x is never followed by the letter **s**.

39

11 The ain and ea Letter Strings

Here are **a** and **i** together in the **ain** letter string.

11A ain
1 again again again again
2 remain remain remain remain
3 explain explain explain explain
4 against against against against
5 It's raining again.
6 The bike remained propped up against the wall.
7 Please explain again.

11B ain
1 mountain mountain fountain fountain
2 captain captain bargain bargain
3 Britain Britain Britain Britain
4 curtain curtain certain certain
5 The captain came from Britain.
6 Are you certain that you drew the curtains?
7 The fountain is beside the mountain.

More **ain** letter strings, although you can't always hear the **ai** sound.

ain

Look out for more **ain** words.

11C   ea
1 ready ready ready steady steady
2 weather weather weather weather
3 feather feather leather leather
4 healthy healthy wealthy wealthy
5 Ready, steady, go!
6 It's better to be healthy than
   wealthy.
7 What's the weather like today?

Here are more **ea** words. Don't expect them to sound the same. An **e** and **a** together can make several different sounds.

11D   ea
1 break break break break break
2 breakfast breakfast breakfast
3 early early nearly nearly nearly
4 instead instead instead instead
5 If you drop that heavy vase
   it will break.
6 He was too early for lunch so
   he had a late breakfast instead.

How many **ea** words can you collect?

Look at the Spelling

Do this work in your spelling pages.

Write the heading: **ain** and **ea**

1. Copy this chart and fill all the words from 11A and 11B into the correct places.

words with **tain**	words with **gain**	other **ain** words
at least 5 words	at least 3 words	at least 2 words

2. *Curtain* and *certain* have almost the same spelling.

    a) Which one has a soft **c**, and what makes the **c** soft?
    b) Copy the following sentence, putting the correct words *curtain* or *certain* in the spaces.
    Are you _ _ _ _ _ _ _ you didn't cut the _ _ _ _ _ _ _?

3. Make up a little story of your own, using these four words.
    captain   bargain   certain   mountain

4. Copy out these words and their meanings, filling in all the missing letters.

    lunch b_ _ _k   stop what you're doing to have lunch
    b_ _ _kfast   meal which b_ _ _ks the night's fast
    (*fast* means *not eating*)
    take a b_ _ _k   have a rest
    b_ _ _kdown   stop working altogether
    b_ _ _k in   go into somewhere you're not allowed
    b_ _ _k out   escape

42

12 Odd jobs for Vowel U

Vowel **U** has lots of little odd jobs.

Q always needs me next to him.

12A   qu

1 quick quick quickly quickly
2 quite quite quite quite quite
3 square square square square
4 quarter quarter quarter
5 Draw a square and divide it into four quarters.
6 I can do that quite quickly

More **qu** words.

I never go out without him.

12 B   qu

1 queen queen queen queen queen
2 quiet quiet quiet quiet quiet
3 squeak squeak squeal squeal
4 squeeze squeeze squeezy squeezy
5 The queen squeezed the squeezy bottle.
6 The mice were quiet – not a single squeak or squeal!

U can also act as a **gu**ard beside letter **g**.

U stops **g** from going soft!

12C   gu

1 guess guess guess guess
2 guide guide guide guide
3 guard guard guard guard
4 guest guest guest guest
5 The guard guided the guest
   to his room, because he
   could not guess the way.

In these words **u** helps **s** to make a **sh** sound!

Sh!

12D   su

1 sure sure sure sure sure
2 treasure measure pleasure
3 sugar sugar sugar sugar
4 usual usual usually usually
5 Do you usually take sugar?
6 It's a pleasure to measure
   the floor — if we find treasure
   underneath!

Look at the Spelling

Do this work in your spelling pages.

Write the heading: Odd jobs for the vowel U

1. Copy this chart and fill the words from Unit 12 into the correct spaces:

qu	gu	su
at least 11 words	at least 4 words	at least 7 words

2. *quite* (sounds like white) and *quiet* (sounds like diet)
   Copy and complete these sentences, filling *quite* or *quiet* into the spaces.

   a) It is _ _ _ _ _ a long way.
   b) He had a _ _ _ _ _ nap.
   c) Please be _ _ _ _ _.
   d) We were _ _ _ _ _ _ _ _ _ _ in the library.

3. The **g** can be hard (like in *guard*) or soft (like in *gentle*) – see Unit 8 for details of soft **g.**

   A **g** followed by **u** is *always* hard (like in *gun* or *gum* or *gull*).

   In some words, **g** has an unexpected **u** beside it to make sure that it stays hard.
   Make up a little story using these **gu** words.
   gun   guard   guess   guide

4. There are seven spelling errors in this extract from a pirate's diary. Find them all.
   Then copy out the passage correcting all the spelling.

   We were shore the treshur was on the island, and we meshured the distance from Shuger Loaf Mountain to the tree. There was an unushal-looking rock and I felt shor this would be the hiding place. I took great pleshur in knocking it over, and there we found...

13 One I or two?

All, full, well and till are words that are sometimes joined to other words. When this happens they lose one I.

13A   all → al

1 always always always always
2 already already already
3 although although although
4 alone alone alone alone
5 almost almost also also
6 I always seem to be alone, although I have almost a hundred friends.

13B   full → ful

1 beautiful beautiful beautiful
2 thoughtful thoughtful thoughtful
3 awful awful powerful powerful
4 useful useful helpful helpful
5 The girl was beautiful and thoughtful.
6 It was awful weather, so her umbrella came in useful.

13C

till → til

1 until until until until until
2 The beautiful princess slept until the prince woke her.

well → wel

3 welcome welcome welcome
4 Welcome to the party!

When **all, full, till** and **well** are not joined to other words, they keep the double **l**.

13D

all, full, till, well

1 After the feast, we all felt very full.
2 We had eaten till we could eat no more, and we didn't feel very well.

all right (two words)

3 all right all right all right
4 Is this handwriting all right?

Look at the Spelling

Do this work in your spelling pages.

Write the heading: One **l** or two?

1. Copy this chart and fit the words from Unit 13 into the correct places.

al words	**ful** words	**til** words	**wel** words
5 words	6 words	1 word	1 word

Can you think of any more words which could go in the first two columns?

2. In 13A, each word is made up of al + another word, e.g.:
    al + ways = always

    Copy this word sum, and write the other four you can make from the words in 13A.

3. In 13B, each word means 'full of something',

    e.g.   beautiful   = full of beauty
             awful   = full of awe

    Copy these two word sums, and write the other four you can make from the words in 13B.

4. | *all right.* |

    This should always be written as two words. (You may sometimes see it written as *alright* in American books, because the American spelling is different from the British spelling. But in Britain it should always be *all right*.) Make up a sentence of your own, using *all right*.

5. *until* and *till*
    These two words mean much the same thing, but note the difference in spelling.

    a) Make up a sentence using the word *until*.
    b) Write the same sentence, putting *till* instead of *until*.

    Does it make sense?

14 Silent Letters

Lots of English words have letters that you can't hear when you say the word.

Ghostly letters, like silent **k**.

14A kn

1 know know knew knew
2 knock knock knife knife
3 knee knee kneel kneel
4 knight knight knot knot
5 Do you know where the knife is?
6 The knight kneeled down on one knee to tie the knot.

And wonderful silent **w**.

14B wr

1 write write writing writing
2 wrong wrong wrist wrist
3 wrap wrap wrapping wrapping
4 wreck wreck wreck wreck
5 I hurt my wrist writing a long story about a shipwreck.
6 We wrapped up the wrong present in the best wrapping paper.

Silent **b** catches out lots of people.

14 C   silent b
1 comb comb bomb bomb bomb
2 climb climb climb climb
3 limb limb tomb tomb tomb
4 lamb lamb thumb thumb thumb
5 He climbed the tree to put
   a water bomb on the bottom limb.
6 The mermaid combed her hair
   by the old tombstone.

But silent **t** is best for catching people out!

14 D   silent t
1 castle castle whistle whistle
2 often often often often
3 listen listen fasten fasten
4 rustle rustle nestle nestle
5 wrestle wrestle hustle bustle
6 We often sat in the castle
   and listened to the rustle of
   the trees outside.

Watch out for silent letters – can you find any more?

Look at the Spelling

Do this work in your spelling pages.

Write the heading: Silent letters

1. Copy and complete this chart, filling words from Unit 13 into the spaces.

silent **k**	silent **w**	silent **b**	silent **t**
at least 8 words	at least 8 words	at least 7 words	at least 9 words

2. The two most important silent **k** words are *know* and *knew*. Copy these sentences and fit *know* and *knew* into the spaces.

   a) Do you _ _ _ _ the way to school?
   b) My friend _ _ _ _ the alphabet when he was two.
   c) I didn't _ _ _ _ her name, but I _ _ _ _ where she lived.
   d) The things that I _ _ _ _ are stored in my brain.

3. Silent letters usually like to attach themselves to a particular letter of the alphabet.
   Copy and complete.

   Silent **k** likes to be in front of **n** (**kn** as in knock).
   Silent **w** likes to be in front of _ (_ _ as in _ _ _ _ _ _).
   Silent **b** likes to be after _ (_ _ as in _ _ _ _ _ _).
   Silent **t** likes to be after _ (_ _ as in _ _ _ _ _ _).
   In one word, silent **t** comes after **f** the word is _ _ _ _ _ _.

4. Three silent **t** words have the word *ten* in them.
   Write them out here.

5. Write a short story of your own including the following words.
   listen   wrong   climb   often

15 sc, ph, ch and Silent h

Some words have strange spellings you have to remember.

In these, the letters **s** and **c** go together to make the sound **s**.

15A   sc

1 scissors scissors scissors
2 science science scientist
3 scene scene scenery scenery
4 muscle muscle muscle
5 The scientist lost his scissors.
6 The Muscle Man looked at the lovely scenery.

And **p** and **h** can go together to make **f**.

15B   ph

1 elephant elephant alphabet
2 telephone telephone phone
3 photograph photograph photo
4 graph graph nephew nephew
5 I took a photograph of my nephew sitting on an elephant.
6 Someone had written the alphabet on the phone box.

Sometimes **c** and **h** can make a **k** sound.

15C   ch

1 Christ Christ Christmas
2 Christmas Christian Christian
3 school school echo echo
4 ache ache ache ache ache
5 chemist chemist chemist
6 We did a Christmas play at school.
7 The chemist gave the teacher some pills for his headache.

15D   silent h

1 hour hour hour hour hour
2 honest honest honestly
3 ghost ghost ghost ghost
4 heir heir heiress heiress
5 At the midnight hour the ghost walks — honestly!
6 The heir to the throne chatted to the beautiful heiress.

An **h** can be silent too!

Look at the Spelling

Do this work in your spelling pages.

Write the heading: Strange spellings.

1. Copy this chart and put all the words from Unit 15 into the correct spaces.

sc	ph	ch	silent h
6 words	8 words	7 words	6 words

2. Write these sentences, filling the best word from 15A into each of the spaces.

   a) The _ _ _ _ _ _ _ _ _ invented a cure for headaches.
   b) We cut the cardboard with _ _ _ _ _ _ _ _.
   c) You have a _ _ _ _ _ _ in your arm called the biceps.
   d) After the play, we moved all the _ _ _ _ _ _ _.
   e) In our _ _ _ _ _ _ _ lesson we learned about space.

3. Draw a picture which includes as many **ph** words as you can.

4. Using the word *ache* make words to fit these definitions.

   pain in the head   =   headache
   pain in the tooth   =
   pain in the back   =
   pain in the stomach   =   (two words)

5. Make up a little story using these words.

   ghost   echo   hour   scene

6. In this letter, there are eight spelling mistakes. Find them all and list the correct spellings.

> Dear Aunty Dot,
>   Thank you for your Crismass present. It is great, onestly. I've always wanted a Kemistry set - now I can do sience experiments on the cat. Thanks also for sending the foto of you and Uncle Mike on holiday. It is beautiful seenery. I will take it to skool to display in our project.
>   Your loving nefew,
>   maurice.

16 The ou and our Letter Strings

The letters **ou** are a common vowel pair.

We're double trouble.

16A   ou

1 double double trouble trouble
2 couple couple cousin cousin
3 country country country
4 touch touch young young
5 My young cousin is always in trouble.
6 He lives in the country and everything he touches goes wrong.

We can **ow** or **oo**, depending how we feel.

16B   ou like "ow"

1 count count county county
2 trousers trousers trousers
3 house house blouse blouse
              ou like "oo"
4 you group group soup soup
5 coupon coupon wound wound
6 The count spilled soup down his trousers.

And **our** is a very common letter string.

16C our
1. four four four pour pour
2. colour colour colour colour
3. favour favour favour favour
4. favourite favourite favourite
5. What is your favourite colour
6. I poured four cups of coffee.

More **our** words.

16D our
1. humour humour rumour rumour
2. harbour harbour armour armour
3. neighbour neighbour neighbour
4. journey journey journey journey
5. There was a rumour that "Neighbours" might finish.
6. The knight made his journey in full armour.

Look at the Spelling

Do this work in your spelling pages.

Write the heading: **ou** and **our**

1. Copy and complete this chart, filling the words from Unit 16 into the correct places.

oub	oup	oun	ous	our
2	4	5	4	11

2. Two **ou** words from the unit are not included in the chart. What are they?

3. Copy these sentences, filling the best **ou** words from 16A and 16 B into the spaces.
   a) You will be in _ _ _ _ _ _ _ _ if you _ _ _ _ _ _ that live wire.
   b) Cornwall is a _ _ _ _ _ _ _ but England is a _ _ _ _ _ _ _ _.
   c) Two people are sometimes called a _ _ _ _ _ _ _.
   d) The knight had a _ _ _ _ _ after the fight.

4. Write out all the **our** words and go over the **our** in a bright colour on each word, to make it stand out.

5. In the U.S.A., many **our** words are spelled **or**. There are several examples in this extract from this story by an American boy. Find them all and write them with the correct English spelling.

> John's favorite color was red so one day he painted his neighbor's car bright red as a joke. However, his neighbor's sense of humor was very different from John's, and he was furious. He vowed that he would never do John a favor again for the rest of his life.

6. Use the following words in a short story of your own.

   four   group   cousin   colour   journey

17 When Should I Drop Final e ?

*Some people worry about whether or not to drop a final **e** when they're adding an ending.*

Well, there's a simple rule that should help you to decide.

17A   Drop e before a vowel
1 come - coming   2 make - making
  come - coming   take - taking
3 live - living   4 hope - hoping
  give - giving   cope - coping
5 The king was making the cakes
  and people were taking them
  and giving them away.

*If the ending begins with a vowel drop the **e**.*

*And of course, **y** is a part-time vowel.*

17B   Drop e before a vowel
1 noise - noisy   2 scare - scary
  noise - noisy   scare - scary
3 like - likable   4 love - lovable
  like - likable   love - lovable
5 He is noisy but he's still lovable.
6 Did the scary story scare you?
7 Someone you like is likable.

But if the ending begins with a consonant . . . .

And not a vowel.

You don't drop the **e**.

17C   Keep e before a consonant

1 hope – hopeful   2 care – careful

hope – hopeful   care – careful

3 hope – hopeless   4 care – careless

hope – hopeless   care – careless

5 I'm careful but he's careless.

6 I'm hopeful but he's hopeless.

Here are some more words where we have added an ending beginning with a consonant.

So the **e** stays put.

17D   Keep e before a consonant

1 late – lately   3 love – lovely

late – lately   love – lovely

2 late – lateness   4 safe – safety

late – lateness   safe – safety

5 The flowers are looking lovely lately.

6 Fasten your safety belt even if you are late.

Look at the Spelling

Do this in your spelling pages.

Write the heading: When do I drop final **e**?

1. Copy and complete.

   You drop the f _ _ _ _ **e** when you are adding an ending that begins with a v _ _ _ _.
   You do not drop the f _ _ _ _ **e** if you are adding an ending that begins with a c _ _ _ _ _ _ _ _ (not a v _ _ _ _).

2. Copy and complete the following chart, dropping the final **e** when you need to do so.

	add **ing**	add **ed**
hope		
like		
cycle		
decide		
clothe		
suppose		
refuse		
scrape		
guide		
measure		
write		
whistle		
telephone		
excite		

3. **ing, ed, y, ful, less, ly.**
   Copy the following short story, choosing the most suitable endings to finish each unfinished word. (If the ending begins with a vowel you'll have to drop the final **e**.)

   Our teacher said our work was care____ and we had to do it again. I tried to be care____ but the classroom was noise_ and it stopped me from concentrate____.
   Afterwards I hope__ that I'd done it all right, but it didn't seem very like____. For a start, my handwrite____ was awful.

18 When Should I Change y to i?

Lots of words end with **y**. When you add an ending you have to change the **y** to **i**.

These are the sort of words where you have to change **y** to **i**.

18A   Change y to i

1 carry – carried   2 hurry – hurried
  marry – married   curry – curried
3 try – tried   4 dry – dried
  cry – cried   fry – fried
5 For dinner we had curried meat, fried eggs and dried fruit.
6 I tried to eat it but it made me cry.

And **y** changes to **i** in these words too.

18B   Change y to i

1 lady – ladies   2 baby – babies
  lady – ladies   baby – babies
3 fly – flies   4 cry – cries
  sky – skies   try – tries
  spy – spies   dry – dries
5 The ladies heard the babies' cries.
6 There were flies in the sties but blue skies overhead.

More words where **y** changes to **i**.

18C Change y to i

1 happy - happiness   2 lonely - loneliness
  heavy - heaviness   busy - business
3 happy - happily   4 tidy - tidily
  heavy - heavily   busy - busily
5 The business man was tidily dressed.
6 Happily, he did not feel any loneliness.

But in a few words we keep the **y** when we add an ending.

Only if it'd mean putting two **i**'s together.

Yes, that'd look silly!

criin

18D Keep y before ing

1 cry - crying   2 try - trying
  fly - flying   dry - drying
3 carry - carrying   4 hurry - hurrying
  marry - marrying   curry - currying
5 He was carrying a box and
  hurrying along the road.
6 The flag was flying, the clothes
  were drying and the baby was
  crying.

This rule does not apply when **y** is used along with a vowel, as in **day, key, buy, boy,** etc.

Look at the Spelling

Do this work in your spelling pages.

Write the heading: **y** changes to **i** before an ending

1. Copy and complete.

   If a word ends in **y**, you usually change the _ to _ before adding an e_ _ _ _ _ _. You don't change the _ to _ when it would mean writing two **i**'s together. You don't change it when **y** follows a v_ _ _ _ _.

2. Copy and complete the following chart.

	change to **ied**	change to **ies**	add **ing**
carry			
marry			
hurry			
cry			
fry			
dry			
reply			
supply			

3. Copy and complete this chart.

	change to **iness**	change to **ily**
happy		
busy		
tidy		
merry		
heavy		
ready		
scary		
spooky		

The Word Party

Loving words clutch crimson roses,
Rude words sniff and pick their noses,
Sly words come dressed up as foxes,
Short words stand on cardboard boxes,
Common words tell jokes and gabble,
Complicated words play Scrabble,
Swear words stamp around and shout,
Hard words stare each other out,
Foreign words look lost and shrug,
Careless words trip on the rug,
Long words slouch with stooping shoulders,
Code words carry secret folders,
Silly words flick rubber bands,
Hyphenated words hold hands,
Strong words show off, bending metal,
Sweet words call each other 'petal',
Small words yawn and suck their thumbs
Till at last the morning comes.
Kind words give out farewell posies. . .

Snap! The dictionary closes.

RICHARD EDWARDS.